Inhabiting love

Poems

Abu Bakr Solomons

First published by Botsotso in 2020

59 Natal St, Bellevue East, Johannesburg 2198
Email: botsotso@artslink.co.za
Website: www.botsotso.org.za

ISBN: 978-1-990922-49-7

The poems©Abu Bakr Solomons

Distributed by

Worldwide: African Books Collective
http://www.africanbookscollective.com/publishers/botsotso-publishing
South Africa: Protea Boekhuis: llendon@proteaboekhuis.co.za and Botsotso

Cover, layout and design: Vivienne Preston

For my mother and father, Fatima and Agmat,
who taught me that love inhabits many places;
and for my grandsons, Zuben-Adam and Zayd.

We must suffer, suffer into truth, and we resist . . . but ripeness comes as well.
Aeschylus: Agamemnon

Contents

I

Inhabiting love

In the morning   7
Womantalk   8
When love laughed   9
Coalition   10
Vanguards   11
Subsequently   12
Unsettled   13
Your stand   14
Shadow boxing   15

II

The geography of remembering

In the old Medina, Marrakech   17
Two women and Als   18
Soles of our shoes   19
The city's fury   20
Georgie's grandmother   21
Cold comfort   22
Kalk Bay   23
Bokaap   24
The day is a red circle   26

III

Signs

Humansdorp   28
Portent   29
Fog   30
Scars   31
The flesh of words   32
Fear   33
Felicity   34

IV

The arithmetic of forgetting

Conversations in early January 36
Winter's witness 37
Love's drudgery 38
Piano tutor: Athlone 39
Heart on the wall 40
The habit of love 41
The arithmetic of forgetting 42
Wigless 43
The logic of nothingness 44

V

Where we live

The enemy is also within 46
Malady 47
Magog, war dog 48
No business as usual 49
Truthdig 50
Turning the other way 51
Dispossession 52
The mystery of the bodies 53
Rise 54

VI

Cleaning

Cleaning 56
Of gates and trees 57
So what can we see through frozen words . . . 58

I

Inhabiting love

In the morning

Morning closes yesterday
as yellow rays defeat reticence.

It is safe to dream again, believe
today will bring fecund arrays of possibility.

Sitting, sipping fresh tea resuscitates,
removes staleness, debilitating inertia.

In the garden, a leafless tree cautions:
forever roams only between winters.

Womantalk

Women talk loudly, confidently;
emptying their hearts and heads,
their fervour enlivens repartee.

Conversations are particularised
or broad, multi-faceted, sprinkled
with mirth; cross-referenced codes
mix lofty allusions with the quotidian.

Guffaws are from belly-buttons,
colouring jibes with sharp words
that skewer drooping cheeks;
dilating pupils portend epics.

Women talk loudly, exuberantly.
But when their voices subdue, it's
a signal – intruders in sight.

When love laughed

You shared my youth
with the Beatles and lyrics

they tenderly smoothed
an awkward boyishness
delivering the sentences
for love's conditions

love laughed in your palms
mischievously
sojourned quietly

for love inhabits or flees
freely to others
whenever it chooses.

Coalition

You collaborate as ardent ally,
duly vigilant against all danger.

You enclose with both arms as if
freeing may precipitate a fall.

Guarding scrupulously on the sides,
your protection comforts, sustains.

The air, earth and sky seal what is
ostensibly an enduring bond.

But doubt always vexes certitude
with its ineluctable interrogation:

Are you truly a friend or furtive foe?

Vanguards

No flowers adorned his funeral. No one wept –
no polite requests for donations in lieu of –
yet as his pupils we sat at his feet observing
how he tended his garden during dark eras.

On stage, in stone-faced solidarity, sat
seven stern men and a sedate woman;
they sang the *Internationale;*
three speakers delivered appropriate eulogies
till a serious comrade dutifully reminded us
it was an *atheist's funeral.*

But then while reading a poem –
tribute about fathers fading –
I caught you wiping tears away;
your heartfelt delivery warming austere ceremony.
Bravely you claimed an opportunity to feel
the alienation departure brings,
knowing political protocol
cannot settle a protégée's sorrow.

And I remembered that time of fervent discussions
in a country of paradoxes as we stridently expounded
about interminable struggles against supremacists
removed from the vigilant watch of all vanguards.

Subsequently

Now that you're gone, I speak fearlessly
for you cannot refute what I am saying
or claim that I am imagining.

- I will say you concealed your angst adeptly
when you listened to me;
avoidance was evident in quick strides.

- I recall you always feared taking risks;
listening to our needs, you brushed
yours away with tomorrows.

- I confirm you shielded us from your yearning;
that behind your smooth self-effacement,
you desired success.

Now that you are gone, I can say you fawned,
hiding a need for affirmation; and in always giving,
blinded us from seeing you.

Death's indiscriminate, decisive . . . leaving us fallen
on a cold floor. But you failed to delude me.
I was always aware that inside you were bleeding.

Unsettled

I am ending a chapter, abandoning
a treasured tie and ignoring
the deafening, facile chatter.

Truth is scoffed. Speeches obscure
contrived to comply with visions
of a milieu's capturing cadres.

So much fawning in the chambers
as the new democracy's old posse
is juggled, portfolios re-shuffled.

The rainbow lies in smithereens
while another dawn slides from slime
into the scrapheap of malfeasance.

Your stand

I thought about the lucid rationale
you expressed, rejecting chemo.

It was early; morning light blending
with the damp leaves of a dying eucalyptus
yet still perfectly stalwart in a soggy earth.

Hidden was a valuable lesson to digest.
I tried to remember each sentence, their words;

This was necessary, you said so resolutely.

On the way to the washing-line your decision
coalesced with the billowing of white sheets:

No more, declared unequivocally.

I lived a rich life, with few regrets.
I want to die in a dignified way, as I lived,

delivered with indefatigable gratitude.

Shadow boxing

There's a gentle yellow beam
seeping through under the door
               across the passage;
a quiet entry before sounds
of footsteps are heard padding
                towards the kitchen.

You visualize a body pacing
to and fro in various spots
               allied to silence;
there's a face and quiet ire
as utensils are banged
              affirming movement.

You imagine someone vexed,
a voiceless being sparring
              in the kitchen;
it's shadow boxing that turns
one in an adjacent room into
             a prodigal nonentity .

II

The geography of remembering

In the old Medina, Marrakech

The allure of your antiquity radiates
from you and your children, Marrakech;
cobbled streets save footprints of invaders.

High clay walls enclose a fortress;
winding enclaves conceal discreet favours
hammams promise perfumed bliss.

An *adhaan* subdues for pious prayers
then your restless, beguiling avenues
pay obeisance to a call from the faithful.

Droves of tenacious lives compulsively
ply their trade on every corner;
caftans and crafts seduce in *Bab Doukalla*.

And in souks robust Berber eclipses French chic,
boisterous bicycles impede our wanderings –
fortitude is palpable in postcolonial charm.

* *hammams* – **hot baths**
** *adhaan* – **call to prayer**

Two women and Als

On the edge of our garden
a hardy als endures winter bite;
tough green foliage glistens
with silvery drow as day arrives.

Its leaves brought trusted relief
for childhood maladies; bore
mother's conviction about their
reliable and restorative power.

For it's a tree that nurtures;
favouring nature's universe, alerts
where we detoured in the name
of progress – profitable enterprises.

There's a sturdy, lone woman who trades
at what's left of the Parare,
promoting assiduously her *duiwelstrek,
wilde dagga and buchu.*

Our als bush protects this panacea
indigenous to rural Ethiopia; cures
while courageously resisting harsh
remedies sold at an exorbitant price.

* *Als* plant Artemisia Afra
** *Parare* the Grand Parade, Cape Town
** *wilde dagga* and *buchu* indigenous herbs

Soles of our shoes

Old newspapers stuffed into my shoes;
craters in the soles since there was
no money to purchase new walkers –

… my tongue still tastes sugar
dissolved with water on white bread;
soggy, yet so deliciously inventive

…oily, milky *vetkoek* fried•
on a neighbour's Jewel stove, spread
lavishly with melon and ginger jam

…outings to the Company Gardens,
feeding peanuts to squirrels;
candy-floss gripped, enchanted

…on Friday after school, making tums –**
melted brown sugar rolled hot in our hands –
with hungry children of St Francis Home.

All recalled when we need to endure,
practise patience, lie and wait for better days;
tying our souls into three fold knots
shielding against dour despair.

• *Vetkoek* – Fried bread rolls
** *tums* – melted brown sugar rolled into sweets when cooled

A city's fury

Mrs D posted me that morning:

They burned my house down last night.
Do you have any blankets for my kids?

I read this browsing in a second-hand bookshop;
rich aroma of percolated coffee streaming through.

I will bring you blankets soon.
What else do you need right now?

She replied succinctly: *Alles.*

Flames consume mercilessly;
raze a humble household into rubble.

Yet what was 'everything'?
Just a small flat, a few pieces of furniture –
ashes made with matches and cans of gasoline.

Reconstructing would take a lifetime of sacrifice.

But again the city's fury may easily flare.
Perhaps tomorrow.

•   *Alles. – Everything*

Georgie's grandmother

Her face like bark of an embattled oak
seemingly empty until she spoke;
then her words melted toughness:
Georgie, her grandson,
roaming the streets again, expelled.

You felt her loyalty, her anguish shielding
this fledgling from ravages of township temptation,
scolding him, offering protection
against further threats,
what seemed beyond control;
you felt her fierce amalgam of love and outrage.

I am fetching him. There is nothing here anymore.
You people can do nothing. Julle is leeg. He must go now,
go where he is a vreemdeling.

So Georgie traipses to and fro like resilient ponies and carts
klip-klop through the streets of Kalksteenfontein;
his granny defying or complying whenever necessary.

Cold comfort

You remember the motherland
in a shelter built for you by strangers
yet deep longing gnaws at your heart;

yesterday's demolition becomes
today's news; your loss suffocates
in makeshift tents and your wounds

bleed in shacks where the well-fed
nurse you as a casualty of solidarity
for their own salvation.

Kalk Bay

I am outstretched, on my back on a wide beach;
a few fishing boats loll in the old harbour
beyond the railway tunnel where three families
revel, enjoying February's summer.

Now this is a coast where periwinkles mysteriously
seem extinct; a concrete platform, where live
skiffle bands gyrated and sun-kissed youngsters once
twisted and shouted, almost buried under shifting sand.

There are no trips of *tickey-round-the-bay* in boats
crammed with carefree passengers rocking fearlessly;
some tunnels are cordoned, wired and locked;
barnacled hulls rust in a greasy pit on the water's edge.

On the jetty, prices for fish are soaring; a few *haarders*
flop on tables with entrails trailing; yes, trading's fierce
as two seals pose obsequiously, perform for off-cuts
tossed their way by two amused and taunting tourists.

Beyond the breakwater, fishermen chug in to dock;
they're solemn; decks littered with empty petrol cans
while memorable fun-train trips to Kalk Bay on Christmas days
wheedle with warm breezes in the afternoon.

In a restaurant above the harbour, pale patrons
stare at each other waiting to be served.
Do they know about Fernandez the fisherman,
a Dirk Poggenpoel, Vincent Cloete or Felix and Sina Florez -

Bhagat Kalan, shoemaker of Windsor Road, Rejaldien?
Old Kalkie sings in photos titillating visitors in a baker's shop
where the amiable owner entices with French doughnuts.
Cuban cigars smell of how a village's patronage has altered.

Bokaap

I will not compose a dirge for you –
our footprints preserved on your cobbled streets.
But I witness a slow demise
far more corrosive than quick erasure.

I see changes each time I visit.
They seem peripheral but the enemy's concealed;
prowling since our pioneers resting
in the Tana Baru battled old *djinns*.
If you remember their ardour,
be still, look around, visit their tombs.

Recall the cane factory that flourished
in Boeta Brayma's backyard.
Where the house stood, there's now a coffee shop
owned by a man with a foreign name.
He sells muffins and *espressos* to tourists
desiring to see the *real* Cape while
relishing the luxuries hard currency buys.

So who will preserve our childhood
when those who remain,
driven by drudgery, necessity,
fall prey to greedy fortune seekers armed
to own a part of our history
by tasting the fare of the children of
querulous natives who strolled
on the shores of *Cabo de Boa?*

The curse of colonial invasions
lures the progeny of conquerors
to the terrains of appropriation.

They wonder at the beauty their forefathers stole,
without beads in their Gucci bags but hard cash
inflated by nefarious trading of recent pirates
on Wall Street.

The beguiling *baas* still plays his tune
in the current milieu duping the gullible.

Gentrification is his ally.

Djinn – *supernatural creatures, not purely spiritual also physical descirbed
in early Islamic theology. They are invisible but are forces of good and
evil affecting the world.*
** **Cabo de Boa** *the old Portuguese name for the Cape*
*** **Baas** *Afrikaans for boss or master*

The day is a red circle

Propped up in his wheelchair,
new calendar on his lap,
he draws a red circle around the date.

Time becomes a number as scribbling
with his wrinkled fingers, this red circle
saves a revolution threatening to escape.

III

Signs

Humansdorp

In bedrocks, aeons of deposits
forged by earth's unfurling,
lies evidence of endless contours
entwined in seams of yellow stone
with the feisty footprints
of bygone migrations.

You said you are hiding there to find yourself –
where a new domain stirs
distanced from duties or impediments.
For what remains are survival tools,
repositories revealing ancient battles;
the past embedded not in words
but in signs of perseverance buried
for us to decipher round campfires.

And so we find vast accumulated histories,
survey mysteries in a landscape,
ferret clues, find pieces to tabulate
and archive fresh inventories
ever closer to the core of ourselves.

Portent

Although it is summer, the sea is murky;
like turgid lies, dead sea urchins bloat becoming flotsam:

a mind sullied with sadness,
impervious to beauty,

swollen bodies of refugees disinterred
on a once pristine coastline.

Fog

There are no signposts;
the white line brightens and fades,
straining your eyes.

You predict collision:
what lurks in the distance?
Anxiety compels deceleration.

The fog clears, a body flashes past;
cars diving towards the source of light,
you sigh –you've been saved!

But just as you navigate easefully,
a brick jolts a closed window:
to find direction nowadays is more than precarious.

Scars

1

Ours, a lethal legacy of scars
mothers and fathers endure desolation,
corrosions plague fragile futures.

2

Contagious curses fester,
a malaise thwarting
settlement, stability.

3

Cells still reverberate with
agonising wails of persecution
through old bastions
hindered by the hereafter of their jailers.

4

We grasp tenuous treaties when presented
by new governors
but bitterness stultifies
feeds the avaricious tastes of new compradors.

5

Imbued ardently with purpose
to honour noble promises for liberty
some battle in burgeoning ghettos
as guns and tik rule.

The flesh of words

We shuffle
languid sunrises and sunsets
in silos of silences.

Death boasts defiantly

in the data of diligent strangers

distanced by austere protocols.

Captives of an implacable isolation
we remain embargoed from
common confluence.

In this confinement it is the flesh

of words we yearn for most, damned

to displays of digitalised endearment.

Fear

Settled in, alone one afternoon,
television ranting about tariffs and wars,
sudden light streams across the floor –
a window prised open? Has a burglar invaded?

I rise, armed to combat the interloper
but only golden sunbeams filter through fretwork
of a room divider.

In uncertain times benevolence
trepidates into menace.

Felicity

White sand spreads to infinity
                    sky
        sea
                        sun

yellow sunlight seeps through
placidly across the water, threads
through pearly pebbles brushing
                    the tips of my toes

            sun
        sky
                sea

behind me two women huddle
on a rock, joking uninhibitedly
pulling expanding waistlines
teasing sagging breasts

                sea
        sky
                sun

I eavesdrop self consciously

nothing in disarray as the day
rotates gently on its own axis

It is how things are meant to be.

IV

The arithmetic of forgetting

Conversation in early January

Staleness of the old year pervades
as we face each other across a table
biting hot toast and decrying
ways of villains, tarnished reforms.

The warm creamy coffee comforts,
enlivens conversation; a sweetness
swirls in the mouth, revives brown
bodies lulled into summer lassitude.

Eradicating a consuming self- loathing,
we slowly begin to grasp possibilities
and exchange turns into new avowals
to demolish doubts and feed optimism.

The future becomes palpable as while
we banter, boisterous, loud youngsters
weave through us, grab empty chairs
in between our proffered formulations.

Driving home, I glance at the notepad
open on the passenger seat: propitious
ideas vivify into varied verdant visions;
a few words excoriate a crippling inertia.

Winter's witness

This year I witness winter winking
through a window in a coffee shop
on the outskirts of our windy city.

A man sitting on a step outside
puffs his cigarette; extinguishes
the butt vehemently with his heel.

Opposite, on the pavement, a young
woman paces; she gravitates closer,
thrusts a note into his hand, scoots.

The waitron delivers a steaming mug
to me and utters: *We are closing today.*
The owner's wife was killed last night.

Love's drudgery

When I hear Frankie Avalon croon,
I see you a belle of the fifties; skirt
billowing over a stiffening petticoat.

I still miss your unquenchable quest
for true love;
                            you acquiesced easily,
putting your head on many shoulders,
daring to risk loss with someone who
was willing to surrender temporarily.

And though promises were often reneged,
and ends of liaisons left you wounded, alone,
you continued to believe
in the drudgery of trivial trysts.

Yes, as men came and left, Love slumbered.
And yet I still miss your unquenchable quest.

Piano tutor: Athlone

I fell in love with you when I was ten,
mastered notes you tutored me on an old piano;
drew keys on a school desk, to practise regularly.

I rendered Omaha in Wright's Pianoforte
with aplomb – pride beamed in your eyes as you
wrote this sublime acclamation in bold lettering:

EXCELLENT!

The word banished boundaries, dear Ava Gardner of Athlone,
where deprivation died for an hour on Tuesdays,
erased diabolical goals of supremacists.

I still play *Omaha* perfectly anticipating approval
from those keen to listen; your commitment shields me, Shirley,
when futility threatens aspirations.

Heart on the wall

A portrait hung on the wall in the passage
of our neighbours' home; these
were the Finnans, who ate fish on Fridays.

So your heart exposed and hands
torn by nails drew me each time
I visited to practise on their piano.

It was a bleeding heart glowing in
an inner lamp that radiated through
a sombre pedantry in the hallway.

There death and freedom bonded in a niche,
a perplexing paradox for one tasked
only to learn a rise and fall of scales.

Many questions followed that death.
Was it you on the cross? Did you die for all of us?
Even me who recites my prayers in a foreign tongue?

Or was it liberation just for some?
And so you defied Caesar's power and the priests
and such devotion speaks of pain.

The habit of love

Browsing through a mall, my grandson
in tow, we bump unexpectedly into her,
exchange pleasantries; and so I seize
an opportunity to share a story with Zayd.

'This is the lady to whom I wrote copious,
love letters and waited anxiously under
a pine tree for our mutual messenger to
bring replies as suitors were prohibited.'

She utters, *Yes, such beautiful letters*
(this was fifty years later), smiles discreetly
because her husband stands next to her;
a curtain raised as the words grew wings.

After goodbyes are said, we walk –
springing with the lyricism of the encounter,
ruffled by love's late harvests –
to where our cars are resolutely parked.

The arithmetic of forgetting

I whispered your name
because you were not there.

Then I added you to a memory
of the time we listened
to James Taylor in corn country.

But the long silence, loss of absence,
slowly subtracted you
from remainders of those hours.

And to counter this, I divide
what is left of all that was
then multiply the smaller parts

to equal a tidy sum which sings
a sweet song no matter what's right.

Wig(less)

I stared at your profile picture;
you were no longer donning a wig.
And it felt that after so many years
I finally saw you bold and true.

Your beautiful dark eyes, contoured eyebrows;
your generous lips –
all seemed so distinct, defined;
unspoiled by a fibred crown.

Then you confirmed how relieved you felt after
almost sixteen years.
How long you struggled with pretence
(what we do to be loved . . .).

You exclaimed how elevating it is to feel rain
pattering without pulling and flattening.
And the dreadful itch vanished,
conquered like a virulent vile curse, exorcised.

Finally you were free to declare:
I am here – no more fraught by turmoil of shame,
re-entering the world with my soft, shiny, ebony crop
laid bare, triumphantly.

The logic of nothingness

I remember coming home
one evening and there was
a telephone call

… and someone said *M. tried to*
commit suicide last night, she's
in hospital . . . and I recalled her
lying still, when I arrived, covered
with a white sheet, and I asked, *Why?*
Her eyes remained closed . . . her
murmuring, *There was nothing to*
be alive for any longer . . .

I felt the implacable certitude
in a simple logic of nothingness
that destroys the pain of longing.

V

Where we live

The enemy is also within

It is not easy to fathom why you strayed when
   I see you in old photographs, courageous,
posing with comrades, your hands and face battered
by ruthless thugs, your clenched fist so defiant.

I wish time had frozen and that bravado
in your snapshot could diffuse
current flotsam of failure . . .

I want to believe that what they propagated about us
   being irredeemably cursed and wholly inept
to deliver our own destinies, were insidious ploys
to consolidate their machinations for supremacy.

You disappointed all of us who wish
to banish the spectre of that history,
their diabolical decrees and edicts . . .

'We are all victims now,' someone commented –
'the oppressed becoming oppressors is inevitable.'
When they pulverised your bones behind prison doors,
did you not anticipate an enemy within?

Malady

When you have vamped your vigilantes,
wisened them to wield words cunningly
and sustain your concealed configurations,
you don't have to swagger bombs, guns or
crude artillery to maintain law and order.

Just oil them well, utilise clichés you
spooned down their throats, alienate them
from the suffering of ordinary citizens
then a million bucks a lackey per annum
clinch as sophistry safeguards their plans.

They will devise strategies, advocate peace
and patience, promote your limp platitudes
like 'Nothing was built in a day' adeptly;
even promote their shrewd gradualist babble
to entice those agitating resistance to retreat.

Later you offer tenders and grand bonuses.
They may feign flashes of guilt but the most
vexed conscience can so easily be assuaged –
money buys things, right, who needs love?
(Even that can be satisfied with a quick grope.)

So the urgency of expectations is subdued
with cool chicanery by these suave bouncers
stemming revolutionary tides. It is then that
an old tuan's words about our malady haunts:
    Makanal Ghuzn

* *tuan – teacher, Tuan Guru, freedom fighter 1792*
Indonesian prisoner of Dutch colonialists sent to the Cape
***Makanal Ghuzn - This is a place of sadness*

Magog – war-dog

In the midst of global disorder,

democracy's racist advocate emerges –
a comic catastrophe, all is lost or won
depending on whose side you are on.

It is a swift coup fanned by fears that
breed insecurity and impropriety:
nothing will be the same again . . .

The serpent is poised in his hole waiting
to poison victims with spurious litanies
of how to rescue the poor.

And in the seat of Empire, a yellow-haired Magog
proselytizes prodigiously about the conquest
of the vile by the valiant:

how tough talk will restore greatness.

No business as usual

Some say there are signs of change in the world,
reckless trade will force known trends to vanish:

those who dominate the corridors of excess
will no longer access conduits stuffed with loot
as dollars and pounds become useless paper
and casualties of financial coups lie gasping
on the marble floors of global institutions,
those brothels of Europe, as promissory fails
and money markets gasp, value becoming virtual
alive only in minds of moguls – streamed shares
shifting from one account to another as frantic
speculators seek immunity from collapse.

A man who slept on the steps of a local bank
crawls to his meagre shelter, modest offerings
                            dangling in his bag.

Truthdig

In the new republic comrades often corroborate:

'That which has correctly been agreed upon ...'
so concluding discussions become an ellipsis.

What was *'correctly'* agreed upon?
Can it be that – *it* - was incorrectly agreed upon?

How was it agreed upon in that way, was it by
consensus or coercion? Perhaps disagreement?
Were some allowed, at that time, to dissent?

Maybe *when* it was agreed upon is inconclusive
but what's important is whether decisions could be
challenged by whoever, without being denounced

a traitor.

Looking the other way

Looking the other way is not turning the other cheek;
                    no one tried to advocate it.

That's a cowardly habit, a mere excuse for not acting,
being safe, protecting your own turf, beliefs.

Falsehood never professes to love anyone.

Looking the other way just protects global scoundrels;
empowers them to placate, saying things will improve,
conniving to erode the courage of the whistle-blowers.

Looking the other way is how corruption sustains itself,
                    weaves into the social tapestry.
It conscientiously shields a new-age barbarism, deceit.

Turning the other cheek is meant to curb the conscious
from being defiled by degradation, not to ignore ignominy.

Dispossession

On a hill near the sea stands a house;
vacant for many years, mouldy relics
decay in empty rooms.

There are rumours that voices echo
through it while stench suffocates with a
putrefying odour and windows are barred.

Old books lie scattered on the floor;
left by those who wrote about past eras,
these dubious tales were interrupted

by the carcass of the master's dog rotting
in the kitchen – a decaying timepiece
for passers-by, who gawking, hurl in rocks.

The future of the house is uncertain.
Still erect with its neglected garden,
it begs for demolition.

Some citizens propose what could
be done: 'Should be cleared!' they cry.
'Homes built for the destitute!'

The mystery of the bodies

The body of Kim Jong-nam was found.
But who killed him?
Was he poisoned? Is there a wound?

The perpetrator(s) vanished, un- identified.
Perhaps they're drinking a few pints
in a downtown bar ?

Africa sang such a dirge for Patrice Lumumba

Now the body lies in a morgue subjected
to scrutiny; no relevant fact is established,
speculation sweeps across many continents .

Africa, again, lamented the slain Matthew Goniwe

Subterfuge pervades unabated. Is it Kim-Jong's
corpse outstretched on the slab? Pathologists
conclude: he dissented and loved Disneyland.

Claiming responsibility for Kim's death will be
a valiant agreement to write your own epitaph.

Rise

Brutal eyes and calloused hearts
in the backyards;

ideals booted out,
anger simmers
as restitution is buried under piles
in the fields of Rohingya and Syria.

At home
degradation is duplicity;
expediency dices
on the dunghills of dire oppression;
party cabals stuff their bags with
stolen cash from municipalities
and dead enterprises.

But soon those who are without rank
shall rise with pitchforks and kieries:

       Nou is ons gatvol! *

*We've had enough!

VI

Cleaning

Cleaning

Renewal waits in a kitchen,
sweeping away last night's leftovers for the
sake of sound housekeeping.

The reward is to see design
in small acts like wiping a table,
preparing a fresh setting.

It is a humble submission
to scour away the dross, without
the usual rules of ritual.

We are quietly guided to perceive how
we may move to clear grubby corners
in dingy passages.

Work delivers a pious homily
with a mop, scrubbed pot, a beaming spirit
on a polished stove.

Of gates and trees

1

The broken gate lies on its back, useless.
Beside it is a pile of bricks, crusted cement.
A fig tree's covered by the debris of leaves
though tiny buds burgeon with summer fruit,
peeking through the contours of branches.

Further down, the guava tree's harvest laughs;
ripeness spreads over the damp lawn as food
and storage for ravenous migrating birds ready
each year to forage bounties after barren winters,
greeting autumn's golden rewards.

The new gate glows in the mellow, yellow sun
for countless exits and entrances to commence;
each history to be etched on its wooden beams,
tough, galvanised frame, beaming for all to see
during impending seasons.

2

Then Shalton, the one who cannot speak or hear,
arrives one cool morning to help me in the garden.
He studies the old gate and shows with his hands
how it could be dismantled, used as panels and bricks
for a room he wants to erect in his mother's yard.

So what shall we see through frozen words . . .

Words are frozen in winter, cold dew on panes
glistens, chills; a lazy sun rises, daybreak fails to
melt the iciness and rigidity; even a warm flow
of breath cannot stir images captive in the heart.

Change arrives dispassionately, like death; the armoury of the present
is indifferent to restive coils unfurling in the gut. What is to be done
is to retreat, wait for vigorous currents to displace stale trends of thought
until our tired muse rekindles and desire dares to flourish, illuminating
love in all the places we may inhabit.

Abu Bakr Solomons worked as a teacher and principal for more than forty years in high schools and primary schools on the Cape Flats and continues to serve the educational community at various institutions on a part-time basis. He studied English language and literature at three different South African universities and abroad.

His poems have been published in **Tribute, Akal** (the journal of the Congress of South African Writers), **Poetry Institute of Africa, Botsotso poetry journals, Sol Plaatje European Union** anthologies, **Sections of Six** (Botsotso), **New Coin** (poetry journal of Rhodes University, Grahamstown) and **New Contrast.**

His debut collection of poetry *A Season of Tenderness and Dread* was published by Botsotso in 2018 and received a commendation from the judges of the Ingrid Jonker Poetry Prize in that year.

Printed in the United States
By Bookmasters